How to Find and Land your

Dream J☑B

Insider Tips from a Recruiter

Mike Wolford

~ * ~ * ~ * ~

How to Find and Land your Dream Job

ISBN-13: 978-0692641408 (Krish Publishing)
ISBN-10: 0692641408

Cover Design by Laura Shinn Designs
http://laurashinn.yolasite.com

Licensing Notes

How to Find and Land your Dream Job is a work of fiction. Though actual locations may be mentioned, they are used in a fictitious manner and the events and occurrences were invented in the mind and imagination of the author except for the inclusion of actual historical facts. Similarities of characters or names used within to any person – past, present, or future – are coincidental except where actual historical characters are purposely interwoven.

~ * ~ * ~ * ~

CONTENTS

~ * ~ * ~ * ~

CHAPTER 1
How to Decide What to Do

The starting point

The first step in any job search is to decide what you want to do.

Some people say that if you do what you love, you will never work a day in your life. That could be true, but what should you do if you don't know what you love in the first place?

My first piece of advice to finding a job that you will be good at and enjoy is to do a great job with the job that you currently have. Doing your current job well will open doors for you to explore other careers that you would not have access to in any other way. It can open doors that will allow you to work in cross-functional teams, take on additional or different responsibilities, or connect you with people who can open doors for you, doors that you could not open yourself.

The next thing to understand in picking a career or changing the one you have is to understand what outcome you want. The result of any job is to produce income. That income will determine the type of housing you can afford, the type of car you drive, and what kind of vacation you have. Once you have an idea of the outcome you want, the trick is to find work that you enjoy that has a reasonable chance of producing the lifestyle you desire.

The good news is that the world is full of options. Do you like to work with your hands? Do you like to help people? Do you like to work in a team? Do you care about the environment? Do you love to speak in front of people, or do you like to write? Ask yourself questions. This is a great opportunity to discover what you really enjoy and what would help you reach your goals. The Greeks used to say, "know thyself." This is the first, and in some cases, most difficult part of picking a path to walk.

I want to be clear. There are many paths to success. Not everyone needs to go to college. There is a growing need for vocational education. The world needs good mechanics, firefighters, carpenters, electrical engineers, morticians, nurses, massage therapists, phlebotomists, insurance agents, dental hygienists, paralegals, construction workers, police officers, surveyors, plumbers, customer service representatives, heavy machine operators, and a host of other professions.

Dollar for dollar your education is the best investment you can make for yourself. Education does not have to be a traditional college degree. The world needs many different skilled professionals.

A guide to self-reflection

If you are reading this, you are thinking about your career and what you want to do. Make an honest list of the things that you enjoy. Do you love to read, do you like to be social, or do you enjoy learning, teaching? Do you like to create things, work with your hands, or think about ways that things could be done better? Make a list of the things you enjoy doing. Whatever it is you decide to do, know that the world needs more people who do that thing well.

Next, think about the type of life you want to have. If money is important to you and you love to teach, ultimately you might find a teaching career to be unsatisfying. Instead, you could blog and teach others about ways to do your job better in the business world. You can look for opportunities to share what you know about your profession with an audience. You can combine your love of sharing and teaching with your desire to do well financially. A career doesn't have to be a zero-sum game of either or. Also, don't limit yourself to being just one thing. In my personal life, I am a father, a son, a brother, and a volunteer. In my career, I am a recruiter, manager, speaker, and writer. You have most likely have heard about thinking outside of the box. Don't struggle to find just one that you fit into.

If you are thinking to yourself, "I'll do anything," you need to understand you are speaking from a place of fear, not power. You are afraid that you will not be able to take care of yourself and your obligations. That is a frightening thing. Try to keep in mind, this too shall pass. When it does, you don't want to be left stuck in a job that you don't like that you cannot loose. Ironically, you can end up prolonging the fear and pain you were trying so desperately to end.

Don't follow your heart

"Follow your heart" is bad advice. If it isn't bad, it is at least incomplete. The heart is a metaphor for emotion, and the emotion most commonly associated with the heart is love. Love is a wonderful thing that makes life worth living, but it rarely puts food on the table. Solely following your heart can lead to having a master's degree in art history while waiting tables and suffering under the crushing and unforgivable debt of student loans. "Follow your mind" isn't complete advice either. People that only follow their mind can end up with high-paying jobs they hate but can't quit.

You don't have to absolutely love every moment of your work. If you got up today and looked in the mirror and said, would I still be doing what I am about to do today if it was my last day on earth, and you answered yes, you are most likely lying to yourself. I'm not certain about you, but if it was my last day on earth, I'd spend it with the people I love. No job, no matter how satisfying, would take me away from my friends and family. Spending time with the people we love is arguably the most important thing we do with our time. It is, however, not a way to make a living. You can enjoy what you do AND make a good living. Remember, you have both a heart and a mind; use them both.

The measuring stick of an idea is fairly simple. Come up with a budget of what you feel you need to make to be content. Can you realistically make that income doing the job you have chosen? If you answered yes then chances are you have found an answer that will work for you.

Remember, "It's a dangerous business... going out your door." Your career is like your life. It is the journey, not the destination, that will shape you. You are very unlikely to end up where you picture yourself. If, however, you have been true to your heart and used your mind, you are more likely to end up being content with the work you have done, the legacy you have left, and the life you have led. Now that you have decided the direction you want to go, it's time to take the first step.

~ * ~ * ~ * ~

CHAPTER 2
How to Network and Build Your Brand

Building a network online

If you have time and you are planning your career, congratulations. You are one of the few professionals taking an active interest in your own career. I want you to start thinking of your career as a business that you own.

For years my advice to job seekers has been to spend 90 percent of your time on your job and 10 percent of your time on your career. So, what are the things that you can do to advance your career and give you the best chance of having opportunity knock at your door?

The best thing you can do for your career is to build a professional network. Networking is critical if you are serious about planning and advancing your career. If you are already actively looking for a job, there are several things you can do in order to help increase your chances of landing a new job.

Using LinkedIn for networking

First, update your LinkedIn profile. If you don't have one, this is a good time to create one. Your LinkedIn profile acts as a great online résumé if you are actively looking for a job. If you have a copy of a résumé already, use the information from your résumé to update your profile.

If you are not actively looking for a job, LinkedIn is your online store for your personal business. Think of it as a landing page for your personal corporation. Remember, I want you to think of your career as your business. Your LinkedIn page is your corporate website and is an important piece of building your personal brand.

LinkedIn also allows you to connect with like-minded professionals. You can join up to 100 groups for free. Join groups that deal with topics that are related to your profession. Build your reputation by answering and asking questions. Ask to connect to the group's top influencers and contributors.

LinkedIn, at its most basic level, is an online rolodex that updates itself. The more contacts you have at your disposal, the more chances you have for opportunities to present themselves. The more people you can reach out to discretely when you feel the time is right to make your next move, the more chances you give yourself of continuing your climb up the corporate ladder.

Using your existing network

The next thing you should do is ask for an introduction or a referral. Don't ask your friends for a job. It puts them in a difficult situation. Often, they aren't the ones that make hiring decisions, and they want to help but often can't directly. What you can do is ask them for referrals. This actually could help them as well as you. Many companies have an employee bonus program, which means they will pay their employees if the company hires someone they refer.

According to a study published in 2014 by CareerXroads, companies fill 20 percent of their jobs from employee referrals. I personally have worked for companies where as many as 40 percent of our jobs were filled by employee referrals. Employee referrals have been the top source of external hires for years. The study further found that a candidate is anywhere from three to 14 times more likely to get the job if they were referred by an employee!

I cannot overemphasize this point. _The best thing you can do to improve your chances of getting the job you want is to be referred by someone who already works at the company you would like to apply to._

The next thing you can do is follow up in a professionally appropriate way. Don't email to confirm an application. If they didn't get your résumé, it would have been because your email bounced. It is professionally appropriate to ask for an update after several days. Reach out to the person who referred you and ask for an update on the state of the job and your application. Keep it simple and to the point. Everyone gets several hundred emails per day, and most of us are not inclined to read long emails. One simple, appropriate question that takes 10 seconds to answer is much more likely to get a response than a long, complicated email.

Establishing your personal brand

Every company is looking for subject-matter experts. Your goal should be to be seen by those in your industry as a subject-matter expert. This is the brand I want you to work purposefully to create. So how can you establish yourself as such an expert?

I first suggest participating in a community blog. While many people choose to start blogs, it can be a difficult process. Typically, it will take around a year for your blog to get a decent following, and that is if you blog every day. Participating in a community blog can help you skip the need to develop followers. An existing community blog already has a following, and it gives you the added benefit of increasing your credibility.

Most blogs encourage active participation in their community. Connect with the owner of the blog and ask if there are any topics they would like covered. In addition to gaining exposure, you also gain credibility. Very few people care enough about their profession to write about it. A final benefit is, over time, many blogs actually pay their writers small fees for writing.

Writing about your profession and getting published in an industry blog or newsletter is the fastest way I know to establish yourself as a subject-matter expert in your field. It's a great first step in building your personal brand.

If you feel truly ambitious, you can also write a book. While not easy, it is now possible for almost anyone to write and publish their own book. This is a great tactic if you have been in your profession for over five years or have worked in a very technical profession. Writing your own book will give you a level of credibility that few in your profession can match. It speaks of a true dedication to your profession and a desire to improve not only your skill, but the skill of those around you.

The research required to write your own book will have unintended consequences. It will force you to think about your profession in detail. It will force you to examine your own process, thoughts, and procedures. If you want to master a subject, teach it.

Also, be open to speaking about your profession. Companies love to hire people that speak, write, or are widely viewed as subject-matter experts. Branding yourself as a subject-matter expert gives you an enormous advantage over your competition.

Imagine you are hiring someone. You have two applicants you really like. They both have about the same number of years of experience and have similar backgrounds. However, one is an active and published blogger on a well-known and respected industry website. Who would you hire?

I know I'm asking you to do "extra" work here, but this relatively small investment of time on the front end can pay huge dividends in your career. Think of it this way. The company Apple is worth about 733 billion dollars. The Apple brand is worth around 98.3 billion dollars. And while your brand is unlikely to be worth close to 100 billion dollars, it is not hard to imagine that it could be worth tens of thousands of dollars. Would you be willing to invest a small amount of time to increase your worth by tens of thousands of dollars?

~ * ~ * ~ * ~

CHAPTER 3
Writing Your Résumé

Formatting and grammar

The first thing you need to do is create a résumé. A résumé should have a few basic elements, including your name, a good email address, and a number to reach you.

A résumé also needs to have the name of the company you work for, your current title, and the dates that you were employed. If you are currently employed, it is acceptable to put "present" or "current" on the résumé for the date. This information should be the first line under the experience portion of your résumé.

A summary of your skills can be included at the top. If you decide to use a summary, make sure you include industry keywords. This will help your résumé rank higher in search results. Most résumés do not have an objective. It is assumed that your objective is to get a job with the company you applied to.

Skills and responsibilities should be listed in bullets underneath the company, name, and title. An example is listed below.

Title, Company Name, Dates (11/13 – Present)

- Skill number one...

- Responsible for...

- Created...

- Increased production X percent over Y period of time.

Style and content

In the bullet points section of your résumé, use action verbs! You want to demonstrate that you are trusted, competent, and results oriented. The next piece of advice is an insider tip. Recruiters are trained first to scan a résumé for keywords. We are trained first to look to match the keywords that represent essential skills with the skills listed as required in the job description. As a general rule, if we see a few keywords in the first few seconds of scanning your résumé, we will continue to read. As someone who has read thousands of résumés, I can tell you we see a lot of fluff in résumés. You are not fooling anyone by listing something like, "provide excellent customer service." That brings me to my next point. What exactly should you write? Think of it this way: if you were at a bar, and you had to explain to someone what you did at your job, how would you explain it?

The point of a résumé is to give the impression that you are a good candidate for the position you are being considered for. There is a difference between saying, "I provide excellent customer service," and saying, "I have won three awards for customer service in the last year based on my customers' feedback."

At the bottom of the résumé is the place for your education. If you have a degree, indicate the name of the institution, the name of the degree, and the date it was earned. The bottom of the résumé is an acceptable place to list additional skills you have acquired that may be relevant to the job you are applying for.

Tips on dos and don'ts

Do not put your hobbies, marital status, or age on the résumé. Those are protected status and do not belong on a résumé.

Do not feel required to put your address on your résumé. It isn't relevant to your search. Getting yourself to work is up to you. If you get the job you apply for, it is your responsibility to get yourself there. You don't want to be rejected for a possible job because the recruiter or hiring manager decides that you won't do the commute. You can put the city and state you live in at the top of your résumé so that you come back in geographical searches, but your address is not required. Another insider tip: when a staffing agency presents your résumé to one of their clients, they remove your address and contact information from the top of your résumé. They simply have your name and their logo at the top of your résumé. I have never heard a hiring manager complain because a résumé was lacking that information.

Finally, have someone else review your résumé. Many recruiters will discount a résumé because of a single typo. Your résumé is supposed to be a representation of your professional experience and a prime example of your best work. At the beginning of the interview process, it is your sole ambassador.

CHAPTER 4
Where to Apply

Indeed.com

Indeed markets itself as "How the world works." Indeed is a great starting point for any job search. It can help you get a high-level picture of what is available in the work place. You can also upload your résumé. Indeed's résumé service works similarly to craigslist. If a company wants to contact you, Indeed sends you their contact request. If you are interested in what the recruiter is offering, you can respond, and Indeed will share your contact details with the recruiter.

Indeed has more internet traffic than any other jobs website in the world. It is the best place to start to a job search. It has a simple interface and allows you to search multiple websites with one easy search. The results are displayed in a way similar to Google search results.

LinkedIn.com

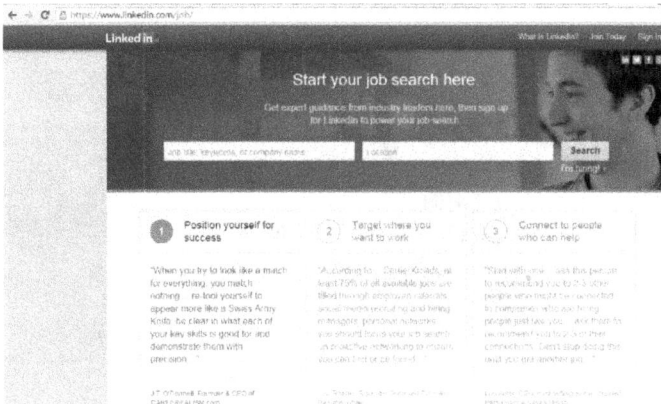

LinkedIn is making it easier for you to find jobs inside your network. LinkedIn job postings will show you if you know anyone inside the company. They have recently partnered with Jobvite to make the process even more streamlined. By reaching out to someone in your network who is employed by a company that has a job posted, you can be referred into that company.

Being referred into a company by an employee is the best way to get a job there. Companies make between 20 and 40 percent of their hires based on employee referrals. Where possible, I recommend taking advantage of LinkedIn's new system that helps you identify people who are in your existing network who can refer you to a new job.

Monster.com

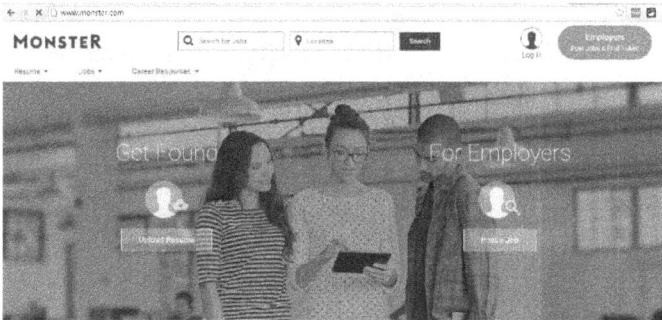

Monster is the original job board. It is best used by college-educated professionals looking for work with mid-cap companies. Monster allows you to post your résumé for free. Employers are able to contact you directly via the information on your résumé. It is a major destination for recruiters and can open many doors for you in your job search. Generally speaking, I would recommend Indeed and

LinkedIn for searching for jobs and Monster and CareerBuilder for being found by them.

CareerBuilder.com

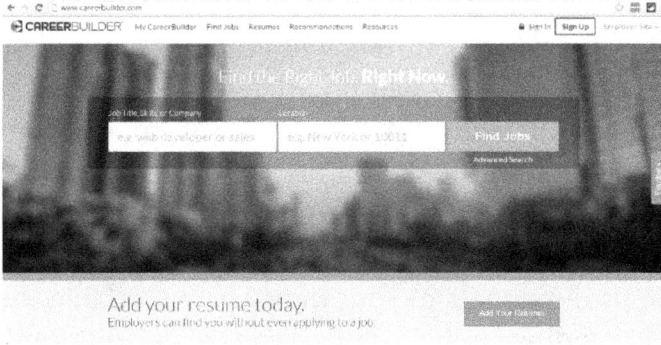

CareerBuilder is a great site to post your résumé no matter what industry you happen to work in. It is one of the premier websites for a job search. Companies pay several hundred dollars to post a job and they pay several thousand dollars per year per recruiter to have access to their database. While they have been around for many years, companies are increasingly turning to job boards like Monster and CareerBuilder to find skilled professionals. It is important to note that your résumé is ranked several different ways by CareerBuilder. One way to be ranked at the top of a recruiter's search is to have recent activity on the site. One of the filters that recruiters use while searching

CareerBuilder is by how long ago you were active. The default setting is 30 days. So if you posted your résumé 31 days ago, your résumé isn't appearing in the majority of searches being conducted by recruiters.

Also, most recruiters will search résumés one of two ways: they will do a keyword search or a job title search. It is important to do your homework and look at a few job postings before you post your résumé. You want to make sure your job title is similar to the one that most of the professionals in your industry use. Using the title "coding ninja," while creative and different, might mean you do not show up on searches where recruiters are searching for "java developer." Also, make sure you have the most common keywords that turn up on your job search on your résumé somewhere. The search engine used by CareerBuilder, and most job board sites, will rank you based on the number of keywords in your résumé that match the keywords the recruiter is searching for. The higher you rank in search results, the more recruiters will see your résumé. The more recruiters that see your résumé, the more opportunities you will be presented with. This becomes increasingly important as you get closer to accepting a job. It is better to have three offers to choose from than just one. To a point, the more offers you have, the more leverage you have to negotiate.

Dice.com

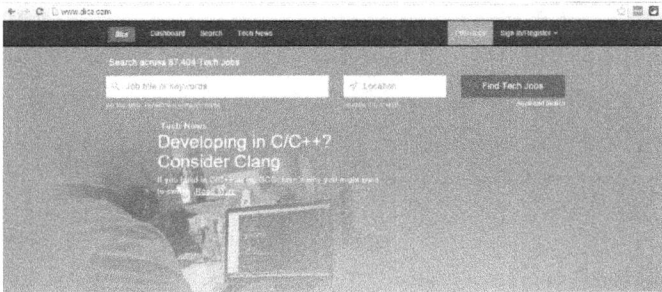

Dice is the largest site for finding a job in the IT field. I spent a number of years as a technical recruiter, and I can tell you from experience that, if given the choice, IT recruiters will turn to Dice before any other job site. If you are a developer, network engineer, or help desk professional, or you are connected in any other way to the IT industry, Dice is a place that you must search for jobs and post your résumé.

Dice works similarly to other job boards. Recruiters search by keyword or title. Often, the keyword searches are technology based. It is important to note that many recruiters do not understand the nuances of the technical terms in IT. For example, many do not know the difference between Java and Javascript. The IT field is ever evolving, and it is difficult to keep up with what selenium is for a QA, or how a dev ops professional fits into an agile development environment. Recruiters are often asked to simultaneously recruit for several different skill sets inside of IT. So while a project manager or scrum master may be able to read and understand your résumé, please remember it first has to make it past a recruiter who may not know that SOA is service oriented architecture.

Snagajob.com

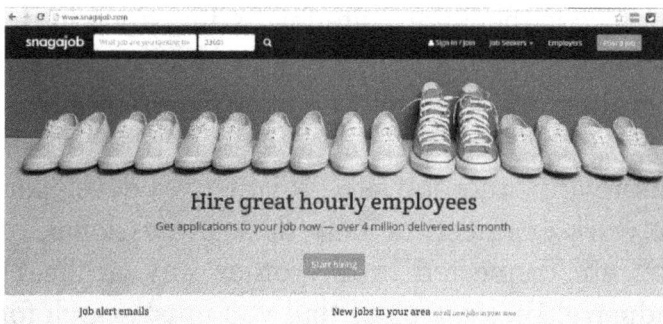

Snagajob is a great site to visit if you are looking for an hourly job. Often, there are thousands of jobs available in retail, security, and warehouses that you simply cannot find on Indeed, and unless you happen to walk by a store and see a "We're Hiring" sign, it can be extremely difficult to find a job opportunity. Similar to Indeed in format, Snagajob makes it possible to search jobs based on location, full-time/part-time/seasonal status, industry, and several other fields. While you are not able to upload a résumé, Snagajob is still the best online source to find a job that pays by the hour.

Here is another insider tip: as you start searching for jobs look for keywords. The common keywords you find in the job descriptions are the ones you need to incorporate into your résumé!

Often, recruiters are working 30 plus jobs at one time. They don't have time to read every résumé, so they are trained to scan for certain keywords. If you don't have those words in your application or résumé, your résumé might be overlooked.

A word of caution. If the job you are looking for requires a CPA, don't lie and say that you have one if you don't. Instead, say "working toward obtaining my CPA." In this way, your résumé will gain the attention of a recruiter for an extra moment. If they read in more detail, it might give you an opportunity that you might not have had.

In some cases, recruiters will try to "sell" their hiring managers on someone who has most of the qualifications required but not all. In cases like this, where a CPA might be desirable, you are giving the recruiter a chance to make a case for you to a hiring manager: "True, this person doesn't have a CPA, BUT they are working toward it. This might be a chance for us to get someone with the same skills, for a little lower salary, and then help them grow into a role." It isn't a guarantee, but it gives you a better chance than you might have had before. Remember, in the job hunt there are no guarantees, but there are ways that you can tilt the odds in your favor. As your job search goes on, go back and incorporate the keywords you are finding into your résumé so that you increase the odds that the right recruiter will find your résumé and reach out to you for an interview.

There are hundreds of niche job boards on the internet, but I've covered the major ones. The vast majority of jobs posted online should be available to you by searching these sites and posting your résumés.

~ * ~ * ~ * ~

CHAPTER 5
How to Use Social Media

Facebook and Twitter

Most companies now have accounts on Facebook and Twitter. Many are opening accounts on YouTube, Instagram, and other social media sites. Increasingly, the reason to have these sites is to engage with you, the perspective employee.

Social media sites like Twitter and Facebook give you an opportunity to engage with a company before formally entering the interview process. If you do not already have an account, create one; they are free and only take a moment to set up. Then I would recommend following companies that work in your industry.

According to a recent study by Simply Measured, 83 percent of Fortune 500 companies have a twitter account, 80 percent have a Facebook page, and 67 percent have a YouTube channel. Interestingly, 30 percent now have a Pinterest board and 20 percent have an Instagram   account (http://simplymeasured.com/blog/new-study-80-of-fortune-500-companies-active-on-facebook-and-twitter/#sm.uq8qjgm8rdsy11hk1gre4jr6ka). The number of companies dedicating resources to social media has climbed over the last several years, and the trend is likely to continue.

For example, Facebook has an estimated 155,000,000 fans, and Coke has 87,000,000. Many of these pages are run by marketing teams and are designed, in part, to attract the most talented professionals to apply for open jobs.

Following companies on Facebook and Twitter can be great ways to find out about open jobs. Many companies are also trying to increase transparency and give more information about what it would be like to work for them.

Don't feel like you need to have a major following on Twitter before you engage with companies. The fact that you have an account is a great start and a possible differentiator. Follow the companies on Twitter that you have an interest in working for, as they will also frequently share stories about what the company is working on. This will give you some good insight as to what is going on with the company before you apply.

Take advantage of this opportunity to get an inside track and learn all you can about a company before you commit to the interview process. This inside information can help you increase your access to opportunities and increase the odds of getting an interview and ultimately landing the job you want.

Don't be afraid to ask questions and get responses from an actual person. Some great questions to ask would be, "What is it like to work for your company?" and, "Are there any exciting new projects in the pipeline?"

Many times, the response will come with an invitation to apply for a job. Most companies want to increase their hiring through social media. The link that they provide you is customized to indicate to an internal recruiting team that you were engaged via social media.

As companies are keen to increase the number of people they hire after first contact on a social media platform, you are actually more likely to get a call from a recruiter than if you replied to a posted job ad and applied directly online.

YouTube and Instagram

Increasingly, companies are sharing their work culture with YouTube videos and Instagram pictures. They are hoping to create an employer brand. This is in part due to a largely unreported change in the labor market. As of this writing, unemployment among college educated professionals in the US is at 2.5 percent and has been for several months (http://www.bls.gov/news.release/empsit.t04.htm).

This has compelled companies to change their approach to talent acquisition. In the past they have been content to simply post their open jobs and interview the people who apply. As unemployment continues to drop and competition for skilled labor increases, companies have decided that it is no longer enough to "post and pray," as we say in the industry. Instead, they are making proactive efforts to attract people to their company who may not be actively looking for a job. Many companies now have a twitter account dedicated solely to talent acquisition and providing information about working at that company.

Other social media sites

Companies are also turning to alternative social media sites in an effort to engage people they cannot find on the major job boards or on the major social media sites. Over 30 percent of Fortune 500 companies have Pinterest boards and Google-plus pages. These sites can be ways to engage with companies under the radar. While there is a smaller number of companies on these sites there is also a lot less traffic, noise, and competition. You actually increase your odds of getting a direct response by engaging over Google-plus vs. sending a tweet to a company that may be getting thousands of tweets per day.

~ * ~ * ~ * ~

CHAPTER 6
The Types of Recruiters

There are several types of recruiters you could be working with, and knowing what type is important because the motivation and methods can be very different. There are five major types of recruiters you can interact with: agency recruiters, executive recruiters, sourcing recruiters, RPO recruiters and in-house recruiters. Agency recruiters are what many people have come to call "headhunters."

Agency recruiters

An agency recruiter is only paid if you get hired. They tend to be very aggressive and very fast paced. Good agency recruiters will be able to connect you with multiple opportunities and often inside information. It is important for you to know at least two good agency recruiters who work in your space. They can provide opportunities that you might not be able to find on your own. Also, typically, an agency recruiter will love you or ignore you. They are extremely busy and are measured on production as well as activity metrics. Agency recruiters are in sales, so when they have a job for you, they will be very engaged. When they don't have anything for you, they are going to seem to vanish. They aren't trying to be rude; they simply are required to be disciplined with their time. If they don't make enough placements, they will be fired. So with an agency recruiter you will either get a lot of attention or no attention. Knowing that in advance will help you understand what to expect when you work with one. From the outside, the agency recruiter's demeanor can appear to be a little cold, but one thing to remember is that recruiter is working to keep his or her job every 30 days.

Corporate recruiters

The majority of the time, at some point, you will be working with a corporate recruiter. A corporate recruiter is an in-house recruiter who works only for that company. They get paid a salary and are not on commission. They are measured on the total number of people they get hired for the company every year, but they have no direct monetary interest in whether or not you take the job.

The corporate recruiter is your true advocate in the hiring process. They want to fill jobs for the company as quickly as possible. They typically work 30 plus jobs at one time. This means that they want to get you through the hiring process as quickly as possible. They have a vested interest in filling the job, and if you have done well in the interview process, they will be a diligent advocate for you to be offered the job because they want to move onto the other 29 jobs that they have to work on. This is also most likely the person who will extend you the formal offer and who will handle salary negotiations at the end of the interview process. It is in your best interest to have the corporate recruiter on your side.

Executive recruiters

Typically, executive recruiters work for a search firm. However, in many cases they are working on a retained search, which means their client has already paid them some money to start the search and they will be paid an additional fee after a hire. While they do have the same pressures as agency recruiters, and in most cases would identify themselves as such, it is important to note some differences. The first is that that the executive recruiter has already received some compensation for their work, whereas an agency recruiter is working solely on commission. Second, an executive recruiter typically works on only senior-level roles. Because the company that has employed them has already committed money to this search and because the search they are on is for a critical and senior-level role, they are going to have a lot more influence on the client as to who they interview. It is important for you, as the prospect, to understand that you have a much higher chance of landing an interview for an executive-level role with the help of an executive recruiter than you would if you applied on your own. Finally, executive recruiters typically focus on a specific niche at the executive level. They know that they might not place you in this role; however, they are likely to have other, similar roles come to them in the future. The good executive recruiters will take extra time with you and try to develop a truly professional networking relationship with you. If you have reached this level in your career, it is worth your time to know a few good executive recruiters.

Sourcing recruiters

Often in the industry, we just call these professionals sourcers. Their job is to seek out and contact professionals who are not actively seeking a job. They are usually seen as specialists in the industry because they are educated in things like Boolean searches, finding hidden contact information, and identifying other ways to reach out to the passive pool of professionals who could be a fit for jobs that their client currently has open.

In many cases, you will get an email on LinkedIn, at work, or even on your gmail from a sourcer. They will identify themselves and typically tell you that they are working on a job that might be of interest to you.

Sourcing recruiters tend to be a little more transactional. They will spend 15 to 20 minutes with you talking about the opportunity and your skills. If they feel there is a match, they are going to ask you for an updated résumé. Once they have your résumé, they are going to present it, along with a short summary of your skills, to their recruiting partner. From there, the recruiter will take over managing the relationship. The sourcer will then return to work searching for other passive prospects.

You should think of sourcers as opportunity knocking at your door. In exchange for a small investment of time and a very low risk proposition, they provide what could be an excellent opportunity for your career.

Testing the waters

There are some avenues to follow if you want to explore your options but aren't really ready to start your search yet. The first way would be to connect with recruiters on LinkedIn. Pick a few companies you would like to explore options with and extend LinkedIn connection requests to recruiters in those companies. An easy way to do that is to use the LinkedIn mobile app. Simply search for the name of the company and the key work recruiter.

Simply press the checkbox and an invitation to connect will be sent. Recruiters will almost always accept your connection requests. This is a good way to start building inside contacts within a company. It is best to have a contact before you need it.

After you have connected with a few companies you have an interest in, the next thing you can do is update your profile. Many recruiters have tools that alert them when people in their network update their LinkedIn profiles. We know it is something people tend to do before they start looking for a job.

Before you update your profile, take a look at a few jobs on Indeed. Search for the job title you would like to have next. Take a look at a few job descriptions. What you are looking for are keywords that are common between the descriptions. These will usually be the keywords that recruiters put into search engines when they go looking for passive prospects.

Armed with the information from your searches, you can now update your profile. Embed the keywords into your profile. For better or for worse, your LinkedIn profile is your online résumé. Do not bombard your own profile with keywords. Instead, strategically place them in different parts of your profile, in your introduction, the bullet points in your experience, and in your interests. Doing so will help make it easier for potential recruiters to find you. I call this experiment the art of recruiter seduction. You are dropping hints that you are open to exploring your options without advertising overtly. It is a very effective way to test the waters before committing yourself to an active job search.

How the system works

Typically, there is a recruiter or sourcer who will contact you first. Recruiters typically are the people who will call you if you post your résumé online, are referred by a friend, or if you apply for a job. A sourcer is the person who will contact you about a job when you have not indicated that you are looking for a new opportunity. Recruiters are hired to manage candidates that are actively engaged in looking for a new job. Sourcers are hired to seek out professionals with specific skills who are not actively in the job market.

Third-party recruiters are usually paid on a per-hire basis. This can be a contract to hire, where they make a margin on your hourly rate after the point you become "converted" and are an FTE (full-time employee) of the employer. The other scenario is where the company pays a flat fee based on your salary. This means it is in the best interest of the recruiter to get you as high a salary as possible.

~ * ~ * ~ * ~

CHAPTER 7
The Interview Process

There are two major types of interviews: the phone interview and the in-person interview. Typically, the phone interview is conducted by the recruiter. After a recruiter reviews your résumé and believes that there is an initial match, they will reach out to speak with you.

Phone interview

Before a phone interview, make sure you are in a quiet place and free of distractions. Typically, the recruiter is not an expert on the technical details of a job. They are going to ask basic qualification questions to ensure that you have a basic understanding of the skills you indicated you possessed. They are going to hone in on your communication skills. Are you able to explain what you do in simple terms? Remember, if you are having difficulty explaining a concept, use fewer words not more. If the recruiter asks you about your salary expectations, you have a few options. I recommend answering with your current or last salary. Then add that you are most interested in exploring the opportunity.

Before any interview, it is important to do your homework. Make sure you visit the company's website, as it is important to know about the company before you interview. Be ready to ask questions based on the information that you have researched. For example, if you read a press release saying that the company has just acquired a new company, ask if part of the growth strategy is to acquire more companies. The recruiter or interviewer may not know the answer, but one thing they will know is that you did your homework. That only can result in a positive impression.

In-person interview

The one thing that most people fail to do for an interview is to be prepared. They walk into the interview not knowing who they will meet, what type of questions to expect, what type of questions to ask and too often not knowing anything about the company they are interviewing with.

Prepare

Before you go for your in-person interview, try to find out from your recruiter who you will be meeting, what their role is, and what kind of questions to be ready for. Also, come prepared with some questions to ask that demonstrate you have done your homework. This is a great opportunity to show the person who is interviewing you that you did your homework without actually having to come out and say it. After talking to hundreds of hiring managers, I can give you another insider tip: when managers hire people, they aren't just looking for someone who can do the job but someone who wants to. If you do not ask any questions, many hiring managers will take that as a lack of interest!

Many of us are told not to boast or seem proud. In an interview setting this can come back to haunt us. The interview is not a time to brag, but it is the right time and place to inform. You need to have some stories prepared that demonstrate your knowledge and abilities.

There are a few common questions you need to be ready to answer. And while a statement answer can be used, it will improve your chances if you illustrate your point with a story. Some common questions to be ready for:

- Tell me about a time you had to resolve a conflict on your team.

- What is your greatest accomplishment?

- What is your greatest weakness?

The first question is especially important if you are being considered for a job in management. At the minimum, you need to demonstrate that you have a process for dealing with conflict. A good response, then, would be to outline your process, share a story that demonstrates it, and then highlight the outcome. For example:

The first thing I do to resolve a conflict is to take steps to avoid it in the first place. I've found that many conflicts arise from a lack of communication or hurt feelings. The first step in my process is to be clear in my communication of needs and expectations. I also have adopted the management style of "praise in public, correct in private." For example, when my team won the award for being the best team of the quarter, I made sure that I sent an email to every member of my team and copied our boss to tell them all how proud I was of them.

The second step I take is...

Continue to outline your process and illustrate it with a story. This will make a positive and lasting impression on the manager. It shows them that you have thought about this before and you have developed a systematic approach to dealing with conflict.

For the question about greatest accomplishment, you should pick a story about how you won a performance-based award. If you have not won a performance-based award, think of a time you received a thank you or any type of recognition for your work.

A story about your greatest strength that ends with you sharing that you had a performance-based award adds validity and credibility to the story. Hiring managers are looking for a pattern of achievement, and when they ask this question, you have your best chance to sell yourself to the manager. I would argue that the chance to answer this question is what you have been working for up until this point. Do not sell yourself short. Come prepared to tell a story about an accomplishment you are genuinely proud of. Detail the steps it took you to achieve it, and keep it timely. Your answer should not be longer than five minutes. Practice your answer so that you remember the steps and timeline of your accomplishment. Conclude your story with the outcome, and then be ready for any follow up questions.

The question about weakness is one that throws a lot of people off. It is a very difficult question! While it may seem clever to answer with a statement like, "I care too much," or "I get too involved in my work," such a response will come across as canned and insincere. I suggest answering the question with a two-step process. First, admit to an actual weakness, and then show that you are working to remedy the situation.

For example:

I don't have a lot of experience in this particular field. However, I have learned quite a lot in the short time I have been working in this field, and I am actually looking forward to learning more. I feel that the fact that I don't have many preconceived notions, coupled with my desire to learn, will enable me to get up to speed quickly and make a meaningful contribution.

Another example:

I have found in the past that I try really hard to please everyone, and at times I have been quiet when I should have said something. I am focusing on learning to become more assertive.

Be ready with a story that illustrates your weakness but highlights your improvement. Do not take more than two minutes to answer this question. Finally, when you have given your answer, stop talking. It can be socially difficult and a bit awkward to do so, but if you do, you will prompt the interviewer to either ask for more detail or move on. Typically, an interviewer will move on if they feel you have answered the question honestly. The worst response you can give is that you have no weaknesses. As a human being, you have them, and if you say you don't have any, they are going to assume your weakness is either dishonesty or a lack of a sense of reality.

First impression

It is true you never get a second chance to make a first impression. My next tip is to show up to the interview 15 minutes early. The administrative staff will notify the manager when you arrive. It sends a non-verbal message to the hiring manager that you are professional, responsible, and serious about the job you are interviewing for.

Life does sometimes get in the way of our plans, and if something does come up that will make you run late for the interview, call your point of contact and let them know!

When you show up to the interview, I recommend you dress professionally, regardless of the work environment. It is difficult to be overdressed for an interview. Also, make sure that your appearance is neat and importantly clean. It seems obvious to many, but over the years, I have been amazed by the number of people who showed up to interviews in dirty clothes or un-showered.

Avoid wearing a lot of makeup, perfume, or cologne. The last thing you want to create is a distraction. You want to avoid putting into the manager's mind that this is what they will have to experience during every team meeting.

Relax

Studies have shown that managers make up their minds within the first 30 minutes of the interview. It does take some people time to relax and come out of their shell. If you know that it will take some time for you to warm up, prepare yourself before the interview begins. If you feel nervous, try breathing techniques or listening to calming music before the interview while you are in your car. If you have a hard time talking with people you don't know, try calling a friend before the interview and talking to them and practicing the interview. This can help put your mind into the right state to be as ready as you can be for the interview.

Remember, if you have made it this far, there is already a general interest in you, your skills, you're your abilities. Generally speaking, you only make it to an in-person interview if they believe you are qualified and able. The interview is their attempt to validate that assumption. You should feel confident and proud that you have made it this far.

If this still seems like a daunting task, try to picture the interview in your mind. Focus on the questions you expect and your answers. Picture things going extremely well and the end of the interview process ending with a statement that you should be expecting a call with an offer or a follow up. Put yourself into a positive state of mind.

Focus

When you get to the location of the interview, turn off your cell phone. You need to focus your attention on the task at hand. Many hiring managers consider it rude to hear your text alarm go off while you are in an interview.

We are often told not to be proud or boastful, as it is a form of bad manners. However, in an interview it is important that you share all of your accomplishments in detail.

After the interview

After the interview, it is important to make some notes. Write down the names of the people that you interviewed with. If they gave you their business cards, take note of their email addresses. It is important to write a thank you note within the first 24 hours after an interview. This is your chance to thank the interviewer and remind him or her of the discussion you had and highlight one or two things you believe that you bring to the table that make you qualified for the job.

Negotiating an offer

The very first thing you need to do is prepare. When you are getting close to receiving an offer, do your homework. Having been a recruiter for a number of years now, I can tell you that many of the people we talk to feel like they are underpaid in their current role. Feelings are important, but having good data is critical. Visit sites like Glassdoor.com and Salary.com to get an idea of what people in your skill set in your area are getting paid. Glassdoor can be especially useful because there might be self-reported data from people currently working at the company you are trying to get an offer from.

Once you have done your homework, you are ready to receive your offer. After you hear the offer, express your gratitude and then follow up with your request. You should say something like, "Wow, thank you for this offer. I'm flattered! I've done some research, and I believe the market salary is five thousand dollars a year more than you are offering. Is there any room for negotiation?" There is no easy or perfect way to ask for more salary. I know it may be uncomfortable for you to ask, or you may feel like the offer is fair. However, I always recommend that you ask! In my career, I've never had an offer withdrawn because someone asked for more money.

It is important to state a reason for your request for additional salary. Hiring managers will typically take into account your current pay when deciding what to offer you. They also are on a budget and are typically trying to get the best people for the least amount of money. So when your recruiter goes back to ask for more salary on your behalf, they are going to need to justify the request to the hiring manager.

Here is an insider tip: at this point, the recruiter is very anxious to get you to accept your offer. They are going to be evaluated primarily on how many people they got hired. They have put a lot of time and effort into getting you to the offer stage, and they want this job filled so that they can get their hire and move on to filling the next job.

Your recruiter also understands that managers want to fill jobs with superstars while paying for interns. In fact, this phenomenon has a name inside the industry. Recruiters say amongst ourselves that the hiring manager we are working with is looking for a "purple squirrel." It helps you to understand that, at this point in the process, your recruiter is your advocate. They understand the market, they know what a reasonable request is, and they are going to do what they can to get you an offer you can say yes to.

It may be that the original offer was the best they could do, or you may receive a higher offer. No matter what the outcome is, express your gratitude to your recruiter. They most likely stepped out of their comfort zone as well to try to get you more money.

Now is the appropriate time to ask questions. A few fair questions to ask: "Is there a sign-on bonus?" "Is there an annual bonus?" "When is my first review, and will I be eligible for a pay increase?" "What is the benefits package?" "How does paid time off (PTO) work?" "Can you tell me about the benefits package?" When considering an offer, it is important to consider the entire package. Sometimes a recruiter has the ability to negotiate a sign-on bonus or extra PTO. Once you have all of the information, it is time to make a decision.

If you have already decided to accept the offer, it is appropriate to accept at this point. If you have competing offers, thank your recruiter for their efforts and tell them you now have to make your decision. It is appropriate to give them a timeline. If you have another offer to consider, it is fair but not required that you disclose it. If you disclose that you have another offer, the recruiter will often take that information back to the hiring manager. Remember, at this point in the process your recruiter wants you to say yes, and if you have another offer they might be able to use this as leverage to get concessions from the hiring manager.

No matter what course you decide to take, inform your recruiter that you will be taking some time to make a decision. Thank them for their work and give them a timeline for when you will make your decision. I always recommend asking for additional salary. Often, the reason for the difference in salary between two people doing the same job is that one person negotiated for more salary and the other person didn't. It is my recommendation that you always ask.

Resigning from your job

Once you have signed and returned the written formal offer letter, it is appropriate to resign. Where and when possible, resigning from your current job should be done in person. Ask for an appointment to speak with your supervisor as soon as possible. You should also write a note giving your formal notice to resign. Keep your resignation letter simple. State that you are grateful for the opportunity you have been given but another door has been opened for you, and you would like to give your notice. In the letter, state when your last day will be. Also, assure your current employer that you will continue in your duties until you leave, and you will make yourself available to train your replacement. While not required, it is standard professional courtesy to give two weeks notice.

Once you have resigned, ask the manager if he or she would like to keep your resignation confidential. It is important to conduct yourself professionally during your transition. The odds are that at some point in your career you will cross paths with some of the people you are currently working with, and you do not wish to burn any bridges behind you. Many companies actively engage in "boomerang" hiring. This means they purposefully target alumni in the hopes that their top performers will return in new roles with new skills. You want to keep that door open. Remember, your job is your business, and you want to give yourself as many opportunities as you can in the future.

Celebrating your success

Congratulations! You have just been through one of the most difficult processes we go through as professionals. Your hard work and dedication have paid off, and you are now in a better role with better pay and an improved career trajectory. It is appropriate and important to celebrate your success. You should feel free to post your new job on social media after you have accepted, signed, and returned the formal offer letter. The interview process, in and of itself, can be a job, and now you've achieved the successful completion of the journey. Now is the right time to gather with family and friends and celebrate the next step in your life!

~ * ~ * ~ * ~

About the Author

Mike Wolford has over 9 years of recruiting experience in staffing agency, contract and in house corporate environments. He has worked with such companies as Allstate, Capital One, and National Public Radio. Mike also published a book titled "_Becoming the Silver Bullet: Recruiting Strategies for connecting with Top Talent_" and also founded _Recruit Tampa_ and Mike currently serves as the Sourcing Manager at _Hudson RPO_. An active member of the Recruiting community, Mike has _spoken publicly_ in an effort to help elevate the level of professional skill. You can follow Mike on Twitter @Mike1178 or _connect_ with him on _LinkedIn_.

www.ingramcontent.com/pod-product-compliance
Lightning Source LLC
Chambersburg PA
CBHW070947210326
41520CB00021B/7087